A Drama in Time

A GUIDE TO 400 YEARS OF RIDDLE'S COURT

Edward Hollis

BIRLINN

First published in 2018 by
Birlinn Limited
West Newington House
10 Newington Road
Edinburgh
EH9 1QS

www.birlinn.co.uk

ISBN: 978 1 78027 555 0

British Library Cataloguing-in-Publication Data
A catalogue record for this book is available
from the British Library

Designed and typeset by Mark Blackadder

Scottish Historic Buildings Trust
(SHBT, www.shbt.org.uk) is a charity dedicated
to regenerating significant historic buildings for
the benefit of others. Each of the properties
SHBT has saved is unique, with its own special
qualities, history and place within a community.
The Trust, which does not receive any core
funding, has over 35 years' experience in
delivering complex projects that restore, repair
and reuse listed buildings; investing in and
regenerating the communities around them.

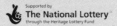

Printed and bound by Gutenberg Press Ltd, Malta

CONTENTS

An Unreliable Guide

Once upon a time at Riddle's Court there was an unreliable guide. With a 'grand proprietorial air', one student later remembered, Mr McKay

points out the very spot where the Bailie breathed his last, and tells how the old worthy entertained Bonnie Prince Charlie and Queen Mary at right royal entertainments . . . Then the old man unbends his back and points up with his stick to a plaster bust of Socrates that a man of unclassical tastes put out in a niche because there was no place for it in his room. 'Yonder,' he says, 'is the image o' Bailie McMorran hi'sel'; it's said to be jist a wonerfu' guid likeness,' and the tourists look up open-mouthed at the rain- and soot-streaked ancient and wonder where the sounds of laughter come from. 'Ou, it's jist they daft student ladies,' says McKay.

Opposite. The true likeness of Bailie McMorran: Riddle's Court in the 1890s.

And he'd shepherd them on.

Mr McKay might have been a joke, but his tall tale tells you everything you need to know about Riddle's Court: about confused tourists, student pranks, famous philosophers, a royal banquet, and a bailie and his untimely end.

Theirs is a long and complicated story.

Built in the late sixteenth century for a magistrate of the town – Mr McKay's Bailie John McMorran – McMorran's Land, as it was then known, became in the seventeenth and eighteenth centuries one of the finest addresses in Edinburgh and home to at least one scion of Scots royalty, if not the Bonnie Prince himself.

When, in the eighteenth century, the fine folk of Edinburgh left their Old Town for the New, Riddle's Court slid into slummery from which reformers repeatedly tried to save it. Engineers cut new streets to bring in light and air, while missionaries, sacred and profane, attempted to tempt the 'human animals who burrowed there' into churches and libraries.

At the end of the nineteenth century, the educationalist and social reformer Patrick

Geddes continued their work. He refurbished Riddle's Court as a student hall of residence and a site for a Scots renascence. His work was continued in the twentieth century by the Workers' Education Association, and it continues today in the education centre that bears Geddes' name.

It's a long and complicated story, and we can hardly blame the unreliable guide for getting confused. Everyone who has occupied Riddle's Court has, like Mr McKay, told the same stories – about banquet and bailie, refined court and reeking slum, town and gown – for their own ends. Those tales have, like the building itself, changed with every retelling.

This guide will follow Mr McKay room by room, working backwards in time to the banquet and the bailie, and meeting along the way all the others whose stories reside in the walls, floors, stairs and ceilings of Riddle's Court.

Right. 'Mr Gepp induces an ancient philosopher to go on the bust': drawing by Louis G. Irvine, student resident of Riddle's Court, 1891.

Opposite. Room by room, back in time: Riddle's Court under reconstruction in 2017.

6

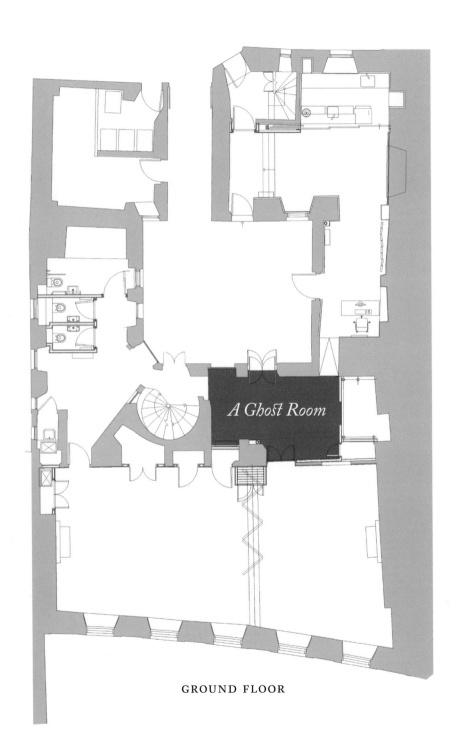

GROUND FLOOR

I

A Ghost Room

The first room in Riddle's Court, the entrance, is also the last.

Created by LDN Architects in 2017, it's a modern sort of room. Look up, and you'll see a glass roof and balustrades of brushed stainless steel. Look east, and a glass lift moves noiselessly up and down. Look west, and coloured light glows under a translucent floor.

This is the entrance to a building with a modern mission: to reach out to school children

A modern reception for a modern learning centre.

Above. By Living We Learn: At work in the Patrick Geddes centre today.

Left. *Vivendo Discimus*: The entrance archway to Riddle's Court.

Opposite. Patrick Geddes: A portrait by the artist Nicky Henderson.

and professors, and to everyone who couldn't be doing with school and never went near a university.

You'll already have seen its modern motto as you came in: it's carved over the entrance archway. '*Vivendo Discimus*', it reads: 'By Living We Learn'.

Hanging on the wall is some modern art: a portrait by the young artist Nicky Henderson of the man after whom the Patrick Geddes Centre for Learning is named. He coined that modern motto a century ago, but this building is much older than that.

It's the sort of building the Scottish Historic Building Trust (SHBT) deal with all the time. 'Conserving the Past: Building the Future' is

Above. St Ninian's Manse restored.

Opposite left. A Ghost Room.

Opposite right. Ghosts of the Ghost Room: The lift shaft under construction.

their motto. They've restored St Ninian's Manse, the only pre-Reformation building in Leith, and they've turned Arthur Conan Doyle's old home at Liberton Bank into a new home for the Dunedin 'second chance' secondary school. Currently they are working to bring new occupations to the Glasite Meeting Hall in Broughton and the Customs House in Leith.

Since 2008, when they were first approached to re-imagine a future for Riddle's Court, they've worked with architects, historians and archae-

ologists to uncover stories at which Mr McKay could never have guessed.

There are traces of those stories in this lobby. The sawn-off ends of joists protrude from the walls, indicating where floors used to be. A cornice appears and, moments later, disappears again, and beneath it there's a fragment of doorframe. The line of a staircase makes its way up the western wall.

These are the remains of lost interiors, and in the recent refurbishment the SHBT kept and exposed them to remind people of all the rooms that had ever been here. At first glance the result is like Mr McKay's stories – an anachronistic muddle.

But it's also a sort of haunting. They used to call one of these vanished rooms 'the ghost room' because it was so hard to find; and its own ghost is still there, halfway up the northern wall. It is only one among many, for this lobby, the newest room in Riddle's Court, is, as we shall discover when we return to it, also the oldest.

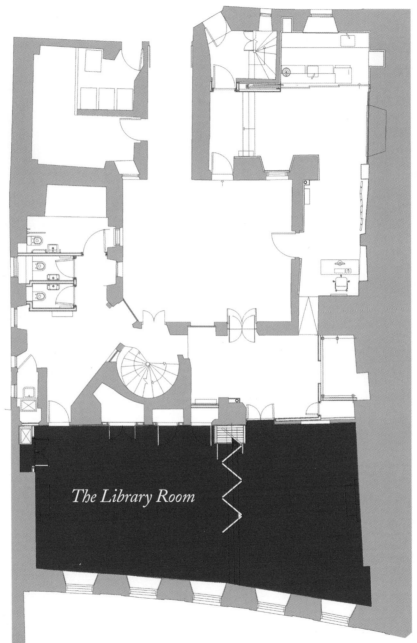

The Library Room

GROUND FLOOR

2

A Library, and a Book

There are no books in the Library Room – and no ghosts either. Or so it appears. Here the memory of the past is alive and well, or at least already perfectly preserved.

In 2017, at the opening of the Patrick Geddes Centre for Learning, the Prince of Wales took tea here, served under crystal chandeliers, against walls of Wedgwood white and blue. At either end of the room, marble mantels sported lions, garlands and palmettes of Grecian correctness. All society was there.

But it had looked very different a decade

A grand room restored: The Library Room.

Right. A royal visitation: The opening of Riddle's Court in September 2017.

Below. A marble mantel: Fireplace at the east end of the Library Room.

Opposite left. The Library Room before the refurbishment.

Opposite right. The WEA at work in Riddle's Court.

before. On 6 October 2006 this room had all the charm of chipped magnolia walls and standard issue strip lights, plastic chairs and disposable tablecloths. Riddle's Court was just about to join Scotland's register of buildings at risk.

The people that met in this room weren't exactly high society either. Teachers, volunteers, activists – they were there for the annual general meeting of the Workers' Educational Association, established in 1903 to 'develop educational opportunities for the most disadvantaged', from help with adult literacy to classes in healthy cooking on a budget.

And this was, they feared, the last time they would meet at Riddle's Court. The ancient building was sliding into disrepair and so were the landlord's finances. The city council was putting it up for sale and it was on the market, the WEA bitterly noted, for a mere £600,000.

Nothing changes at Riddle's Court, they remembered, for six decades before, in 1946, the council had acquired it for an even merer £1,700. There had been no electricity in the building then, and John Middlemiss, who had grown up there, reminded the WEA how 'bath nights meant that cold water had to be heated on the

gas hob and the "black-leaded" open range fire' under the windowsill.

But the building had potential, and when, after a decade of repairs, the WEA started teaching there in 1966, *The Scotsman* thought it ideal for its new purpose:

Centrally situated, and well equipped with gracious rooms of various sizes, Riddle's Court lends itself well to acting as a focus point for the development of all types of cultural activities for older students.

The WEA ran classes in those gracious rooms for the majority of the year, and during the Fringe Riddle's Court played host to the Diverse Attractions – a drama and performance group specifically aimed at the people of Edinburgh.

Once upon a time, the WEA remembered, this hall had been hallowed by the first public appearance of Maggie Smith. In 1979, the Cambridge Mummers had played plays about Sylvia Plath and Antonin Artaud.

They'd put on plays about Riddle's Court, too, and the stories it had to tell: John McGovern wrote the mystery *The Riddle of Riddle's Court*, and in 2005 C.S. Lincoln's *Gentlemen's Bairns* told the tale of the bailie and the banquet.

The 2006 Fringe programme described Riddle's Court as 'a venue where reason prevails', but that doesn't seem likely, given that they were hosting in those gracious rooms *The Bacchae* and the Ladyboys of Banknock.

Next year, the WEA agreed, no Diverse Attractions would come to Riddle's Court. Most likely, the building would have become a boutique hotel or a shop for tartan tat. It was, after all, happening everywhere else on the Royal Mile.

The people who met in the Library Room on that day knew they couldn't stop the sale. They believed they couldn't do much to influence

Warming up—and cooling down—for the Festival

The Fringe comes to Riddle's Court: Maggie Smith and fellow actors.

the future, but that didn't stop them discussing what that future might be.

It was a future, they believed, that should be firmly rooted in the building's past. They proposed 'a Living Museum, as Patrick Geddes would have envisaged, to advance learning to all ages', a place in which 'future generations can appreciate the history and activities housed in it', or a Patrick Geddes Centre, where his approach to learning could be practised in today's context.

It was, on the face of it, idle speculation, for a small charity like the WEA didn't have the financial resources to purchase, restore and maintain an ancient building like Riddle's Court.

But the WEA did have resources at their disposal that a developer or a hotelier, for all their millions, did not: education, people to educate, and a history of centuries of education on this site to celebrate.

Of course there had been Patrick Geddes, but before him, the WEA remembered, in this very room, there had been a library for the 'mechanics' – the working men – of Edinburgh. It was they who had installed the elegant Georgian fireplaces at the ends of the room.

And so, on 6 October 2006, the Workers of the Education Association decided to use their greatest resource – the workers themselves – to write a book of their own: the story of their home, to ensure that 'those selling it and any future owners were made aware of its significance'.

It was a project true, we shall discover, to the spirit of the Mechanics' Library and to that of Patrick Geddes. The WEA's director, Joyce Connon, recalled: 'They did not call in a team of professional historians; instead they designed a project which enabled local people to direct and carry out the work.'

The workers took photographs, wrote poetry, searched through census returns and read David Hume. Louisa Humm wrote 'How to be a Building Detective', while Frances Mercer wrote 'The Ballad O' the Bailie'. Together they built a library of memories, some lived, some historical, some imagined: an epitaph for the Library Room they were about to lose. Mr McKay would have been proud of them.

On the last page, Wendy Jones wrote a short poem:

Far left. The WEA AGM in Riddle's Court, 2007.

Left. *Vivendo Discimus*: The cover of the WEA Guide, 2007.

Riddle's Court and Riddle's Close
(Old Stone, New Wood)
MacMorran and Geddes and David Hume,
Canteen Caretaker: 'Upstairs to Rooms.'
Kings and Queens and Danish Nobles
But the council needs pounds and dollars
*   and roubles.*
Vivendo Discimus: By living we learn
Not for much longer:
Riddle's Court and Riddle's Closed.

You can guess what they called their book, for by living, they had learned.

That publication is the predecessor of this guide, just as the Workers' Education Association is the predecessor of today's Patrick Geddes Centre for Learning. It was also its progenitor, for even as they wrote up their past the WEA secured the future of Riddle's Court.

They started a process of renewal that ended up involving a wider group of local residents, academics, community groups, students, gardeners and craftspeople working under the name of Friends of Riddle's Court Edinburgh –

FORCE. Riddle's Court, it turned out, had more, and more energetic, friends than its dilapidated appearance might suggest.

It was proposed, and agreed with Marilyne MacLaren at the city council, that the Scottish Historic Buildings Trust could step in and take over the building, and conjure, from its own past, a future for Riddle's Court.

The story the WEA had assembled of the life and times of Riddle's Court made it the perfect candidate for intervention, and so, in 2011, the SHBT acquired the lease and started their work: fundraising, investigating and planning. By 2015 they were on site, and by 2017 the work was complete.

In the Library Room, strip lights were taken down and magnolia paint scraped away, mantels restored and chandeliers hung. The twentieth century, with its disappointments and its conflicts, was cleaned away and the room made to seem as if it had always been there, ready, as Riddle's Court had always been, for a royal visitation.

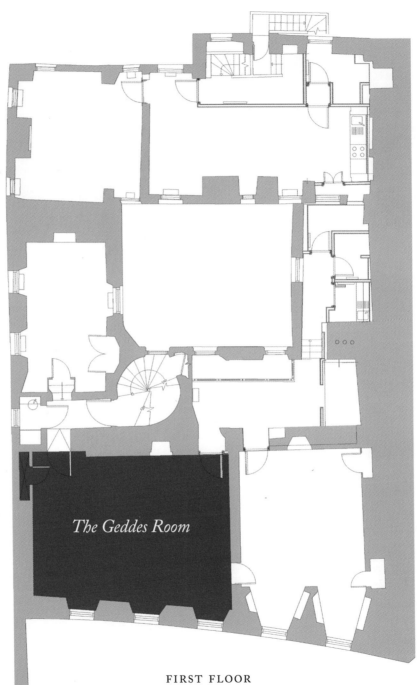

The Geddes Room

FIRST FLOOR

3

A Painted Ceiling

Patrick Geddes haunts the building today, just as he haunted the Workers' Education Association in 2006. To meet his ghost, we must leave the hall and take the turnpike stair up to the Geddes Room on the first floor.

The ghost is on the ceiling. In fact, it *is* the ceiling: an elaborate confection of portraits, emblems, heraldry and histories, as complex and confusing as the stories of Mr McKay. The bailie and the banquet are both there.

One can imagine that this room, with its dark, grained panelling, is where that story happened, too; and the ceiling certainly feels like it was painted in the time of the bailie.

In the north-west corner, the scales of justice hang over books of sacred and secular law. In

Geddes' ghost: The painted ceiling of the Geddes Room under restoration.

Top. A room fit for a banquet: The Geddes Room.

Above. Rhetoric and Grammar; Medicine; the Physical Sciences; and Law, Sacred and Profane.

Opposite. A Thinking Machine: The ceiling of the Geddes Room today.

the south-west, an owl flaps over grammar and rhetoric. In the south-east, twin serpents twine round the medics' staff; and in the north-east, the tools of the physical sciences surround the globe they study. All knowledge is there.

But a small palette painted in the north-east corner of the ceiling records that it was created by the painter Thomas Bonnar in the 1890s for one of the first student halls of residence in the city. This hall was the creation of Patrick Geddes, and on this ceiling, above the table at which the students who lived here ate, he had painted his educational manifesto.

It's an experiment. A thinking machine, Geddes might have called it. It's certainly laid out like the ones he used to make for his students.

Botanist by training, activist by inclination,

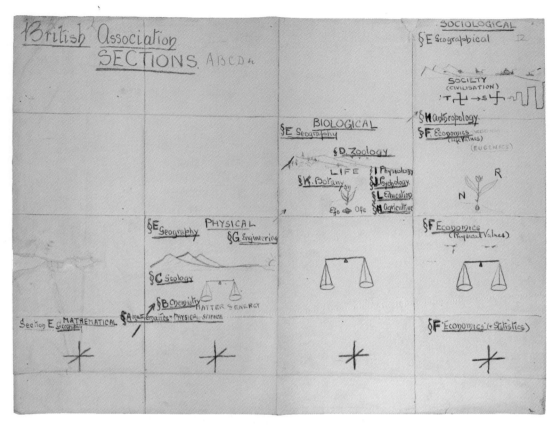

positivist by conviction, and property developer by necessity, Patrick Geddes was too mercurial and disruptive ever to occupy a comfortable chair in the University of Edinburgh, but it didn't stop him interfering in how they housed their students.

Riddle's Court was intended to be:

a sort of co-operative society, a kind of Anarchist community, innocent of regulations. Each member is, or should be, guided by a law within himself, not one imposed from without.

Geddes believed that students should live together, benefitting from the informal and interdisciplinary education 'afforded by the unconscious mental giving and taking ... when the men meet at the leisurely dinners and around the fire of an evening'.

And this room was key to that 'giving and taking': that's why all the four faculties are painted on the ceiling. Geddes was more interested in the conversations that might be had between the medic and the divine, poet and engineer, than in anything those disciplines might have to say on their own.

It sounds like a modern idea, but in fact it's a renaissance conception, and on this ceiling there are portraits of scholars from the sixteenth century as well as the nineteenth. Initials commemorate prominent forbears, and cartouches record the histories of the University and of Riddle's Court itself.

In each cardinal direction, an hour glass divides and unites centuries, for, under this ceiling, the students' conversation was not just about, or with, the present or the future: it was informed by the past. One student later recalled an evening that might have been a renaissance banquet:

Opposite. A thinking machine: Sketch by Patrick Geddes.

This page, top left. The bailie and the banquet: Cartouche on Bonnar's ceiling.

Top right. The centuries, brought together on one ceiling: Panels from the ceiling of the Geddes Room.

Above. Four scholars: The Arts, the Humanities, Medicine, the Physical Sciences.

The heart of the thinking machine: The arms of the City of Edinburgh.

would, at the end of their education, join the doctors and scientists and lawgivers and poets, past and present, who were painted above them, to become its future citizens. 'Thought does not exist by and for itself,' he continued. 'It arises from life, and widens in proportion to its range . . . *Vivendo Discimus*.' You'll know what that means by now. It's painted on the ceiling, too.

There's one group of forbears that didn't make it onto Bonnar's ceiling. It's an irony, for forty years before it was painted they had been sitting in the Library Room just downstairs, expounding the same ideas.

When in 1854 the Edinburgh Mechanics' Subscription Library moved to Riddle's Court, it boasted 850 members, who were able to access 17,000 books for the small sum of a shilling a month.

At a public meeting marking the occasion, its patron, Lord Ardmillan, informed the assembled 'mechanics' that education

> *has done and is doing good work; and we recognize with satisfaction the result, not only in the good order and the tranquillity of the country, but also in the preparation of intelligent workmen for the duties and rights of citizenship.*

The local MP, Duncan Mclaren, was less patronising:

> *He did not claim superior intelligence, honesty, or education for the working classes; but so far as his observation had enabled*

devoted to a burlesque study of Primitive Man (Very vividly illustrated!) and the Evolution of the Ballad Dance – a feast of fun which those who saw are not likely to forget; nor will the picturesque scene in the quaint old common-room of University Hall, Riddle's Court, with its grotesque disguises, prettily costumed dancers, and ring of laughing spectators, quickly fade away from remembrance.

In the centre of the ceiling there is the castle: the crest of the city of Edinburgh, for Geddes built his student halls right in the middle of the Old Town. 'Our true University is thus in the city,' wrote Geddes. 'Nay, more, it *is* the City.'

And, he hoped, the students who ate there

The bailie and the library: 'McMorran superintends the bigging'. Illustration in the 'Proceedings relating to the Heritable Property of the Mechanics Library'.

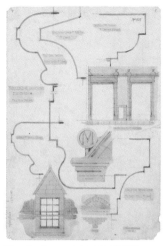

Care for the past, and the future: Detailed drawing by Stewart Capper and R. Traquair for repairs at Riddle's Court.

'The Toast was Drunk': drawn on 20 November 1890 by Louis G. Irvine, student resident.

him to judge, he claimed a greater freedom from prejudice than was to be met with in any other class. They had less to unlearn than the classes above them.

The head of the town council, the Lord Provost, preferred to avoid politics, reminding the mechanics 'that they were traversing the same courts that had been visited by some of the greatest people in Scotland three hundred years ago'. There had been a banquet here, he told them, and a bailie who breathed his last.

Geddes inherited from the Mechanics' Subscription Library not just a house of education but also a sense that being in a building could be an education in itself. It's something the WEA and the Patrick Geddes Centre for Learning have inherited from him a century and a half later.

It's what made them all treat Riddle's Court with such care.

'I would respect and preserve examples of the honest and characteristic work of each and every period,' Geddes wrote, and the beautiful drawings prepared by his architect Stewart Capper for the occupation of the building illustrate how much effort was taken to understand, to preserve and to bring 'renewed usefulness and beauty' to the ancient fabric.

If you walked into the Geddes Room and thought it was where the banquet took place and the bailie breathed his last, you won't be the first or the last: it is the product of a project both ancient and modern, radical and conservative. Its legacy is felt today not just in the ancient building but in its new purpose, now, as then.

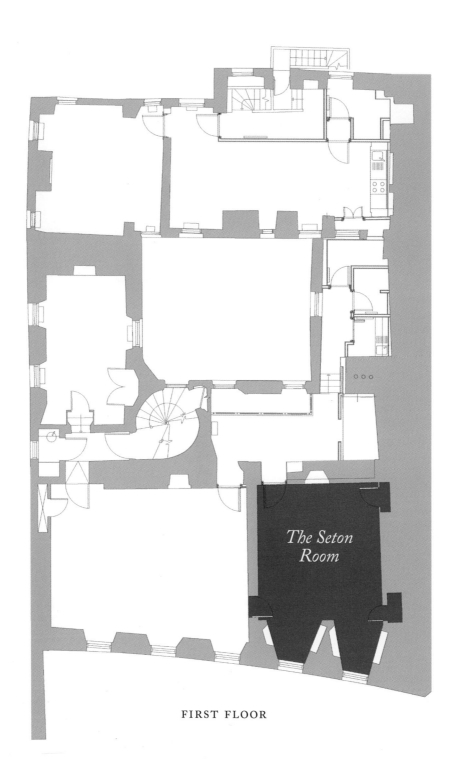

The Seton
Room

FIRST FLOOR

4

Window Seats

Geddes called his interventions into the ancient fabric of Edinburgh 'conservative surgery', and nowhere is this conservatism more evident than the room through the door at the east end of the Geddes Room. The Seton Room, it's called, because it's thought that the ceiling was made in the early seventeenth century for Alexander Seton, Chancellor of Scotland.

The mathematician John Napier dedicated his treatise on logarithms to Seton, and one can imagine them in this room, in the window seats, looking out at the gables of Victoria Street, discussing art and alchemy. It's where Geddes' students used to come after dinner, inspired by the ceiling above them to do the same, in mind and body.

Or so those students might have imagined. In fact, these window seats are modern: 1890s

The Seton Room today.

Seton's ceiling.

Above. *Mens sana in corpore sano*: Pugilism and discussion in the Seton Room, drawn by Louis G. Irvine, 1892.

Left. A place for looking at the city: The window seats in the Seton Room.

suture for surgery that was anything but conservative, for sixty years before Geddes' students sat in here in the evening gloom this room was hanging in midair, above the heart of a vast building site.

In 2016, builders taking up the floor unearthed the scar: an enormous beam dividing the square body of the room under Seton's ceiling from the area that contains the window seats. It was made of several lengths of timber nailed together – a way of achieving strength and length in an age before the steel beam – and it ran along the line of what must once have been a wall.

That beam had been inserted to hold the building up when that wall was demolished. We know when it happened. In February 1836, the Edinburgh Plans and Works Committee met

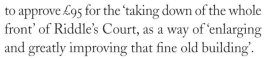

A building site: The Seton Room under reconstruction in 2016.

Victoria Terrace under construction.

to approve £95 for the 'taking down of the whole front' of Riddle's Court, as a way of 'enlarging and greatly improving that fine old building'.

'Improvement' was something of a euphemism, for in fact Riddle's Court was sliced through, from top to bottom. It is a miracle – or perhaps a tribute to the strength of the flitch beam – that the building, let alone Seton's ancient ceiling, survived at all.

Dramatic as it was, it was only a tiny part of a radical proposal from the architects William Burn and Thomas Hamilton for a new street running from the Grassmarket up to the Royal Mile. Its creation involved cutting through all the tenements that ran from the Lawnmarket down to the Cowgate, slicing open the living rock upon which they stood as well as the buildings. Most of them disappeared: Riddle's Court was a lucky survivor.

And the new street – Victoria Street – was only one among many such 'improvements'. At its head, George IV Bridge vaulted over the houses of the Cowgate to Chambers Street, cut through a warren of small squares to South Bridge, which leapt back over the Cowgate. Finally, North Bridge flew over the new railway station, dug out of a drained loch, to the first and greatest improvement of them all: the New Town, built in open country by council decree in 1752.

This was rethinking the city on an industrial scale.

Ostensibly, all those bridges and tunnels and streets were designed to enable wheeled traffic to move around a city that, as Daniel Defoe wrote, suffered 'scandalous inconveniences' as the result of its picturesque situation.

But they had economic purposes, too: the

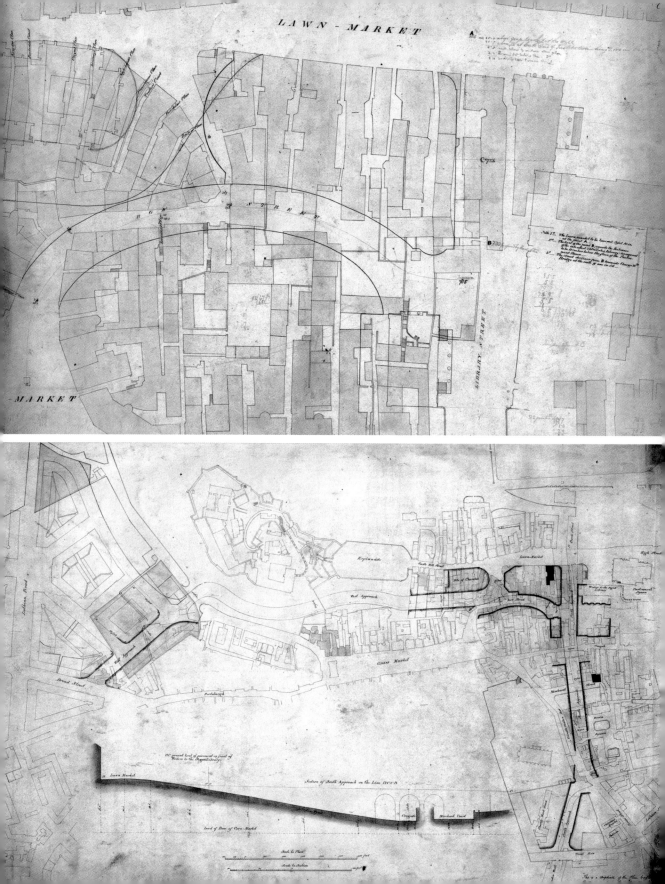

LAWN - MARKET

- MARKET

Opposite top. The new street: Burn and Hamilton's proposals for Victoria Street, showing where demolitions would take place.

Opposite bottom. Radical surgery: Burn and Hamilton's proposals for George IV Bridge and environs.

Left. Nineteenth-century engineering meets the Old Town: George IV Bridge from the Cowgate, 1860.

Below. A city re-engineered: Edinburgh in 1830, General Post Office Directory Map.

new, improved Edinburgh was designed to facilitate the movement of goods, services and capital. It was a cog in the great machine of Empire and free trade, Enlightenment and industrial improvement. The ancient character of Riddle's Court was sacrificed on the altar of efficient manufacture.

'Think Global, Act Local' wrote Geddes five decades later, and that's just what had happened at Victoria Street.

But the window seats he had installed to disguise the scars of the operation suggest, however, that it hadn't happened quite as he might have wished.

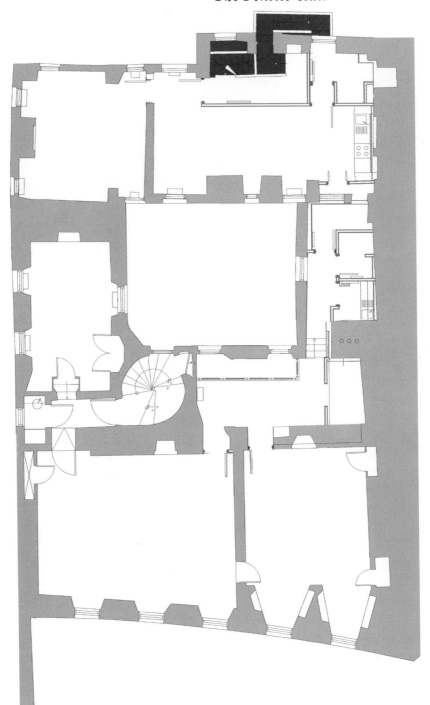

The Pentice Stair

5

A Winding Stair

All that was solid had melted into air, but many disapproved of the improvements.

Writing in the 1830s, Lord Cockburn expressed his impatience with these naysayers. 'They let their picturesque taste get so sickly that they sigh over the destruction of every old nuisance or encumbrance,' he wrote, and he despised their hypocrisy: 'They never try to live among these fragments, nor think of the human animals who burrow there.'

Burn and Hamilton hadn't worried about those 'human animals' too much. The purpose of their improvements was principally economic, but it was hygienic too; for it swept away what they called 'the wreck and rubbish of past centuries, sinking fast under the pressure of their own weight, receptacles of filth and hotbeds of contagion'.

But Patrick Geddes had thought about them. When he'd started working for the university, he'd moved to the Lawnmarket in 1886 to live among them, and from then on the chief purpose of his experiments with town and gown was to improve the lot of those 'human animals' he

A squalid conglomeration: Tenements in the Lawnmarket in the mid nineteenth century.

35

On the tourist trail: Postcard of the stair at Riddle's Court, early 1900s.

A royal stair: Prince Charles opens Riddle's Court, 2017.

found burrowing in what he called 'the most squalid conglomeration . . . in the old world'. To meet them, we're going to leave the Seton Room. Back in the Ghost Room, we'll pass ghosts of the numberless garrets and bedsits they lived in. We'll go down into the courtyard and out of the pend. Look up and you'll recognize a picturesque stair, hanging high on the wall, so idiosyncratic it's become the emblem of Riddle's Court.

Like the window seats in the Seton Room, it's a 1890s invention: a replacement designed by Geddes' architect Stewart Capper for another vanished stair. Below it, stubs of doorframe and quoin indicate the building that contained it. Look carefully, and you can just see the ghost of the original steps on the wall.

In December 1872, the missionary George McNaughton entered that stair for the first time. He was on his way to save souls, or at least to ask the people who lived there why they weren't going to church. He and his successors recorded whom they met and, more than a century later, their diary was passed to the SHBT.

36

A picturesque feature: The stair in 1903.

The ghost of the other Riddle's Court.

There were the usual helpful old ladies, but there were slammed doors too: from the Shearers, who exclaimed they 'could never think of going into a neighbour's house to a stair-meeting' to the Catholic McMahons, who told him that they were of 'the real church'.

'As this stair is dangerous at night,' wrote McNaughton, 'it was deemed advisable to stop here.' Indeed, when they returned, the missionaries soon discovered the truth of the Edinburgh saying that when people 'come down in the world they rise in the stair'.

At the top lived Mr Armstrong, who, it was well known, drank. Just below him was Mrs Morrison, whose 'husband has been drinking, takes things out of the house and has lost his work'. She couldn't come to church, she explained, because he had sold her respectable clothes to pay for his habit.

The lack of a Sunday suit was a repeated complaint: the lamplighter Mr Hammond and his family had not attended church for four years: 'With the clothes I have,' he said, 'I am almost ashamed to go clean my lamps.'

The stair in 1930: The line of the original stair on the wall below can be clearly seen.

The stair before the stair: Riddle's Close in 1854. The arch into the inner courtyard is there, flanked to the east by the corbel above the diagonal entrance doorway.

'I looked at him,' wrote McNaughton, 'and it was true enough. He seemed clothed in a few oily rags.'

In February 1874, Mr Glass told them he would attend church if only he could obtain the right clothes. A striker, he had only five shillings a week from the union to feed his family. He would, he said, send his daughters out to work to supplement this income, but his wife had broken two ribs on the stairs and the girls had to stay at home to keep house while she recovered. By May, one of their babies had died. By November, Mr Glass had started to drink.

There were thirty-three households at that time within Riddle's Close – or thirty-three with whom the missionaries were able to engage. The 1881 census records, at the same time, 247 inhabitants. That's nearly eight people in every flat.

These people lived four decades after Hamilton and Burn had claimed that their improvement would sweep away 'the wreck and rubbish of past centuries', but the progress of history had passed these people by. All those stories of bailie and banquet certainly had little to offer them, and so did the buildings they had left behind.

Geddes' instinctive reaction to the engineered improvements of the 1830s might have been revulsion, but on this occasion he found himself, despite himself, agreeing with Burn and Hamilton.

One rainy day in the 1890s a journalist followed him into Riddle's Court:

'Do you wonder Edinburgh is renowned for its medical schools?' asked the Professor grimly, as he darted in and out of these foul alleys, explaining how he was demolishing this and reconstructing that – at once a Destroying Angel and a Redeemer.

And at Riddle's Court, Geddes acted Destroying Angel. His Town and Gown Association quietly bought the apartments and evicted the undesirable tenants, one by one. Then, when they had purchased them all, they demolished them, and to mask the violence of the act covered the scar with Capper's picturesque stair.

Surgery, however conservative, is still surgery, and in this corner of Riddle's Court, surgery it had to be.

A lamplighter at Riddle's Court.

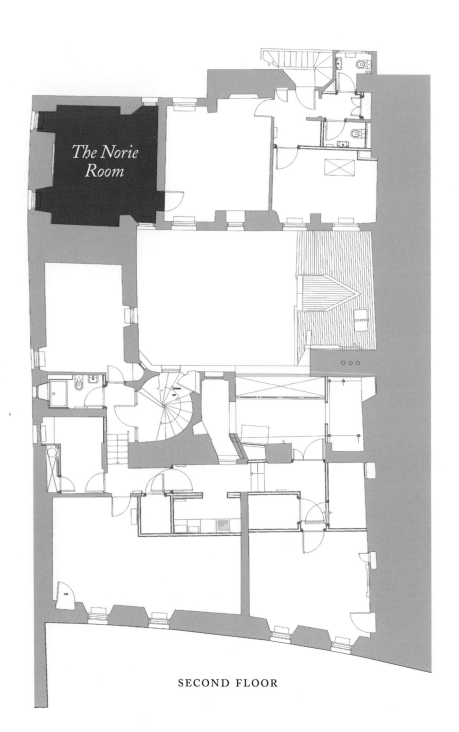

The Norie
Room

SECOND FLOOR

6

A Panelled Room

At the top of Stewart Capper's winding stair, there are fragments of a much grander past.

In the first room there's a grand fireplace. The second, the Norie Room, is panelled and painted a luminous green. On the ceiling is a rose of roses, thistles, lions and cherubs, and a number – 1684 or 1648, it's hard to tell.

In 1871, a gentleman paid a visit to these rooms and found an old bookstitcher 'brisk as a bee, clean as a new pin' living there. He wouldn't find what he was looking for, she said.

One previous tenant had stolen a picture panel from the overmantel, she said, another had sold his to an American. Then, she continued,

a fishcadger occupied the Royal Apartment and finding it rather dark for his taste, and being a tidy kind, he bought white paint and painted up the whole room. Had the owner known, the panels might yet have been saved, but ere he became aware of the fact, a still lower tenant than the cadger succeeded royalty, and, as fuel was dear, and

A once grand fireplace: The west wall of the Norie Room before restoration.

The Norie Room today.

the wood panels handy, he laid the better half of them on the fire . . .

The elegance of the empty panelling that remains reminds us that before the improving engineers had carved it up, and the mechanics and the students had taken it over, Riddle's Court been quite a different sort of address.

It certainly had different names: Royston's Close, for Sir James Mackenzie of Royston, who lived there in the early eighteenth century; and before that Smith's Land, for the Lord Provost, who'd bought it in 1630.

In that time, the householders' roll read like a guest list for a royal banquet. There was John Clerk of Penicuik, Member of Parliament; Sir Roderick Mackenzie of Prestonhall, Justice; Sir Thomas Stewart of Balcashie; Sir Archibald Mure, Provost; Sir Robert Stuart of Tillicoultry, Justice; and Sir Thomas Mackenzie, the Earl of Cromartie.

Lowliest among them was a certain David

The picture of sophistication: David Hume, painted by Allan Ramsay, 1766.

'The Great Princess': Anne, Duchess of Buccleuch, with her sons.

Hume, philosopher, who moved in 1751 into a part of the tenement, newly built by the wright George Riddle, that we would now call 'affordable housing'. His modest household, he wrote, consisted of:

> *a head, viz., myself, and two inferior members, a maid and a cat . . . With frugality, I can reach, I find, cleanliness, warmth, light, plenty, and contentment. What would you have more?*

Grandest among them was Anne, Duchess of Buccleuch. She styled herself 'the Great Princess' and insisted to her dying day that she be served on bended knee.

So she might: she'd appeared at court in 1662 aged eleven. Within a year, she had bagged the most sought after bachelor there: the Duke of Monmouth, bastard son of Charles II.

'He was a lovely person, had a vertuous & excellent Lady that brought him great riches & a second Dukedome in Scotland,' wrote the

Left. The panels, hidden behind paint and paper.

Opposite. A political emblem: The Norie Room ceiling rose of roses, thistles, lions and crowns.

diarist John Evelyn, but 'see what Ambition and want of principles brought him to.' For, when his father died, Monmouth raised a rebellion against his uncle, the new King James, and failed, fatally.

His wife survived him and retired for a while to Scotland to enjoy her treasures, among which was a *pied-à-terre* in town, at Riddle's Court. She spent little time but a great deal of gold on the place.

In 1715 she purchased three windows of the most modern sash-and-case design for the dining room, the lady's bedchamber and the antechamber. In 1717 she acquired two marble mantels, and had the dining rooms painted in green 'over in oyle'. In 1729 she had a new rose fixed to the ceiling of the high dining room and panels painted for the walls.

The names of these rooms tell a story: not many tenements had high dining rooms or antechambers. In the time of the Great Princess, garrets and chambers were knocked together to make the palatial apartments, ready for royal banquets that she and her high-born tenants would have known at court.

The ceiling rose tells a story too, for palaces are always political.

The lions refer to the Scottish Crown, and the thistles and roses to the unions between England and Scotland. We know that all of the occupants of Riddle's Court who could voted for the Union of the Parliaments in 1707.

But the date is ambiguous: 1684 is the date in which Sir Roderick Mackenzie acquired Riddle's Court; and the ceiling could commemorate his purchase.

A green bower: The Norie panels installed in the National Museum of Scotland.

But the '4' is fixed back to front, and it could therefore be read as 1648: the year, in the Scots Calendar, in which Charles II became king of Scotland and England. Indeed, 'C2R' appears elsewhere on the ceiling.

The Great Princess, after all, had every reason to love the old king, her father-in-law, who had made her a duchess, and to hate his successors, who had executed her husband.

And that leaves us with the painted panels, for whatever the old bookstitcher believed in 1871 some of them survived the fishcadger and his fellow tenants. They were discovered behind layers of wallpaper in this room during building works in 1963. You'll find them down the road, in the National Museum of Scotland, where, empanelled in walls of luminous green, they occupy the ghost of this very room.

When it contained them, that chamber, buried in the dense fabric of the city, must have felt like a green bower in an elegiac landscape of meditative figures, distant cascades, ruins and purple mountains.

There's a painting in the National Gallery

An imagined Edinburgh: James Norie's view of the city from the west, 1745.

by the same artist, James Norie of Edinburgh, in 1745, transformed into the same sort of landscape: the castle is a folly glimpsed over a lake, the city itself the merest jagged wisp behind.

It's a fantasy.

But it's a fantasy that, within thirty years, got built – in James Craig's New Town, and its successors – 'thinly inhabited, and that chiefly, by persons of rank', with their classical temples, bridges, glades and palatial apartments.

It's a fantasy that led to the flight of all those aristocrats and judges from the Royal Mile and Riddle's Court, plunging them into the social and economic decline from which subsequent generations found themselves working, time and time again, to rescue them.

The apogee of elegant living in the Old Town, the Norie Room contained the seeds of its own destruction. A work of art for living in, it was destroyed by the people who lived in it: the fishcadger who painted the paintings over and the anonymous man who fed their fragments into the fire.

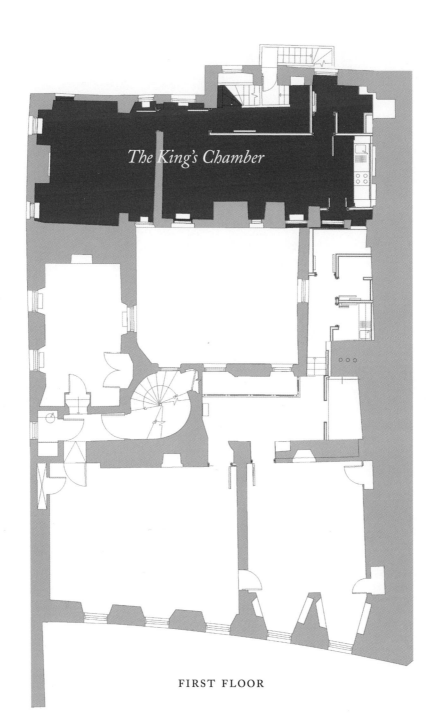

The King's Chamber

FIRST FLOOR

7

Bailie and Banquet

Down the winding stair again, there's a very different apartment.

It's actually an apartment, to start with: with a bedroom, and a sitting room, and a long table to sit and dine at.

Crude heraldic emblems emblazon the dark timber ceilings. The green men, the crowns and the double-headed eagles in the King's Chamber emerged in 1963 at the same time as the Norie panels upstairs. Builders discovered the simpler beams in the larger hall outside in 2016.

They made another less glamorous discovery downstairs. Go to the loo and you'll find a gigantic chimney, large enough to cook a banquet in, complete with a bread oven. For years, no one had known it was there.

These discoveries are connected – and not just by a party wall – for they tell the original

A royal apartment: The King's Chamber today.

49

Opposite. An apartment fit for a king.

Above. Heraldic emblems: The ceiling of the King's Chamber today.

Right. A room in the process of revelation: The King's Chamber during the construction works of 1963. The painted beams on the ceiling are just emerging from above the plaster.

A ceiling hidden for centuries: Restoration work on the beams of the outer room of the King's Chamber in 2017.

story of Riddle's Court: the one Mr McKay used to tell, about the banquet and the bailie, breathing his last.

Once upon a time, in 1590, the Queen of Scotland, Anne of Denmark, made her entry to Edinburgh. She rode from the Grassmarket up the West Bow under a purple cloth of state, in a golden coach, accompanied by knights and ladies dressed in cloth of silver and gold.

By the old city gate, the party stopped. A globe descended from the top of the arch. It opened in four quarters, and from it emerged the provost's son, dressed as an angel, holding a Bible and the keys to the city, which he gave to the Queen.

She may not have noticed the shops on the corner. They belonged to the Bailie John McMorran, a merchant with nine ships, plying wine, wax, pistols and salmon across the sea. Behind his shops he was building a new house,

almost a palace, 'for the decouracyon of the toun', or so he said.

Seven years later, the Queen was back, this time with her husband, the King, and her brother Ulrich, the Duke of Holstein. He'd come on a diplomatic mission to secure European approval for the succession of James VI to the English throne upon the death of Queen Elizabeth.

He was there incognito, but ten days after he arrived the bailies decided that their town should entertain him and, on 24 March, they set aside the staggering sum of £1,103 17s 8d to do so. There were to be two great meals, one on 30 April and one on 4 May.

They spent £184 on sugar, £212 on 'fowls wylde and tame' and £136 on two 'punschions' of wine. There was a boiled ham and a Dutch ham, venison and quail piles cooked by the King's patissier, four stone of salt butter and a stone of fresh, five dozen eggs, milk, three barrels

The Great Chimney is discovered in the construction works of 2016.

of Bordeaux, five gallons of claret, a tun of English beer, forty-four barrels of ale, rose water, linseed oil, half an ounce of saffron, cinnamon and, most exotic of all, thirty fresh oranges.

There were trumpeters, minstrels, an upholsterer to hang the tapestries and guards for the gate. Messengers were sent to summon the guests, and compensation had to be found for the bailie George Geddes, who fell and hurt himself during the banquet. Timber was brought up from Leith, along with 600 nails for the construction of a new gate, temporary bakehouses and boards for cooking and eating on.

There was, of course, only one house magnificent enough for such a production: the newly built house of the Bailie McMorran.

Even then it's hard to imagine how the whole production could have fitted into Riddle's Court.

It's worth remembering that renaissance eating was a hierarchical affair in which only the royal guests would have sat down. James VI was known for repartee when he ate; but his son Charles used to make his courtiers stand and watch him, in silence. Not just that, commoners waited in the hall outside, while the royal party sat in a special 'chamber of dais'.

The emblems on the ceiling of the King James Room support the idea that it was that 'chamber of dais'. The crown is the Crown of Scotland, and the double-headed eagle is the symbol of the Holy Roman Empire, of which the Duke of Holstein was a prince. The green men recall the oak-clad savages who supported the arms of Anne of Denmark.

To no one must the occasion have seemed more hierarchical than its host, the Bailie Ninian McMorran. Not only had an army of courtiers invaded his home; not only did he have to stand and watch politely as they drank themselves into a stupor; but his family were victims of a mis-

The double-headed eagle and the Crown of Charlemagne:
The arms of the Holy Roman Emperor, Rudolf II, at the time
of the banquet.

An whit will be, will be."
A muckle beam they lifted up
And gied the door a dirl
A lad look oot the windae sma'
"Gin ye ca on a'll gaur ye skirl"
The men dung on. The door it cracked.
The laddies filled wi dreid.
"Noo haud yir haund ma baillie bold
Or a'll shoot ye through the heid."
The men dung on. The hinges gied.
Young Sinclair taen the lead.
A pellock whustled through the air.
McMorane drapt doon deid.

The bailies of the town took young William
Sinclair into custody for murder, but he was a
nobleman – his father was Chancellor of Caith-
ness – and he argued that as a nobleman he did
not fall under their jurisdiction.

Both sides appealed to the King, and the
King decided that Sinclair should be tried by a
court of his own peers. Naturally, they acquitted
their boy, and five years later he was pardoned,
and knighted, by the same King.

Deprived of justice, the McMorran family
were at least left in peace to share John's pos-
sessions between them.

There were French black gowns lined with
velvet, and one of Florentine serge; 'breikis' and
doublet in velvet, satin, taffeta and worsted, hats
of felt and taffeta and crepe. There were musical
instruments, 'hagbuttis', two cutlasses and a
short sword.

There were pots and pans in the kitchen,
beds, tables of oak and walnut, an almirah and

carriage of justice, because of their social status,
at the hands of their guest of honour, the King.

Three summers before, Ninian's brother, the
Bailie John, the man who had built the house,
had been summoned to the Royal High School.
The pupils had barricaded themselves inside
and it was McMorran's job to batter the door
down to get them out.

What happened next is best told in a ballad
written four centuries later by Frances Mercer
for the WEA guide:

McMorane came wi armed men
A merchant douce wis he.
"We'll ca' the door in first, ma men

Anne of Denmark around the time of the banquet in 1595 by Adrian Vanson.

James VI around the time of the banquet in 1595 by Adrian Vanson.

chests of cypress wood, chairs with backs, and low stools for women, brass candlesticks, three deer heads, a dresser, an iron chimney and an English Bible.

And there was, of course, the house that John McMorran had built; and when they were grown, in 1616, his two sons divided it between them, Ninian taking the south side, and George the north, with their uncle, Ninian the Elder (the bailie of the banquet), maintaining a share.

Divided from one house into several, McMorran's great house changed from a palace into a tenement, and of course they started squabbling among themselves soon enough: tenement dwellers always do.

George blocked up the entrance to the courtyard with a timber 'ravel', and Ninian took him to court to make him take it away. He knocked through walls he shouldn't have, and Ninian

made him block the openings up again.

And they squabbled with their neighbours, too: as tenement dwellers still do.

In 1614, Ninian the Elder sued John Mure for digging a ditch that prevented his sewage from flowing freely down to the Cowgate. In 1639, George took his neighbours to court for pouring filth out of their windows onto the roof of his own dwelling. In an age without sanitation, these were urgent problems, especially for a tenement inhabited by around fifty people.

The consequences were predictable. In 1624, the plague arrived in the city with a sailor from Gdansk. Ninian the Younger lost five of his six children and finding himself in the Great Tenement almost alone he decided to sell it.

And so ends the story of the house of McMorran, of the banquet and of the bailie breathing his last.

A Mighty Wall

8

The Ghost Room, Again

The story of the banquet and the bailie has all the qualities of a folk tale, and a folk tale it has become: retold again and again in the ways in which people have, over centuries, re-used the building in which it happened.

We know how the story ended, but we still don't know how it began, for we still don't really know what John McMorran actually built in 1590.

His will tells us a little about his house: it describes a chamber of dais and a more private room called the 'bairns' chamber'. Above the bairns was a 'high chamber' and, elsewhere, a gallery, a hall and a kitchen.

It doesn't sound like the whole building. But we can only guess, for writing is writing, and building is building.

We'll need to return to the room in which we started. It's a ghost room, after all, that contains traces of all the rooms that have ever been in Riddle's Court, even the ones that were there before it existed.

For John McMorran didn't start from nothing: there were buildings on this site before. Part

A mighty wall: The south side of the Ghost Room.

City meets country: Edinburgh in 1647, in the Gordon of Rothiemay Plan. Riddle's Court can be seen by the West Bow, facing south over open gardens.

warren of turnpikes and garrets to the north.

This, some think, is what's left of the King's Wall, built around Edinburgh in 1450. Fragments of it survive elsewhere, below Johnstone Terrace, and in Tweeddale Close. It certainly matches those fragments in might.

The King's Wall was no longer in defensive use by 1590, but its presence was still felt: it was the barrier, for instance, at which Anne of Denmark received the keys to the city in 1590, and McMorran's title deeds refer to it as the southern boundary of his property.

That would mean that McMorran's court was carved out of a dense warren of rooms inside the city wall, and that on the other side, overlooking open gardens, the grander library and Geddes and Seton rooms were added as the 'country retreat', later, by someone else.

It's not the only medieval mystery hidden in the Ghost Room.

On the west side of the room, the glowing glass panels in the floor conceal a stair: you can see traces of the next flight scribed onto the wall above. Look out of the window and you'll see that it lines up with the eastern wall of the entrance pend and, beyond it, to the close that leads out onto the Lawnmarket.

Running dead straight, it's a line that divides Riddle's Court into two equal halves on every floor.

We've come to know this place as a court, a miniature palace, a community of people, a college of students; but that line reveals, beneath all that, there was originally another reality.

Look at any map of the Royal Mile, made

of one of them, we think, still forms the south wall of the ghost room.

A huge structure, it rises vertically, rather than thinning, as most walls do, towards the top. It divides the roof in two and mouldings at the high level suggest that once it was, on the ghost room side anyway, outside. It divides two very different sorts of spaces: the grand rooms facing south onto Victoria Street, and a smaller

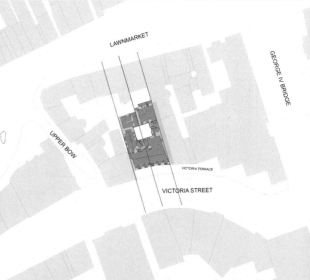

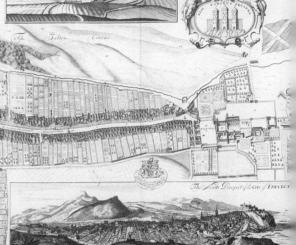

Top left. A hidden stair: The original access between Riddle's Court and the Cowgate revealed during the construction works of 2016.

Top right. An underlying pattern: The red line indicates the possible line of property boundaries that pre-existed McMorran's construction of Riddle's Court.

Above. A pattern of properties, 1647: Tenements of land in the Edinburgh view of Gordon of Rothiemay.

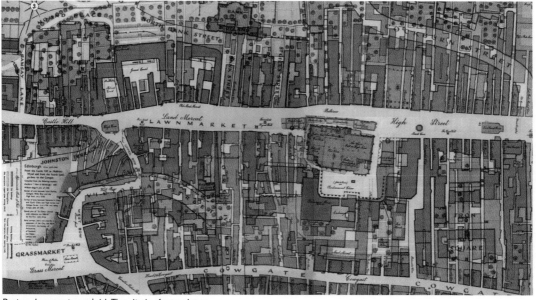

Past and present overlaid: The city in 1695 and 1945.

at any time, and you'll notice that the distance between every wynd and close is about the same as the distance between that line and the plot boundaries of Riddle's Court.

It's the oldest pattern in the city: centuries older than the King's Wall, or the banquet, or the bailie, for that regular spacing of entrances and property boundaries was decreed by King David I when he founded Edinburgh in the eleventh century, dividing one tenement – that is, landholding – from another.

The best image of King David's Edinburgh was drawn by Geddes' son-in-law, Sir Frank Mears, eight centuries later.

There are still tenements and lands on the Royal Mile, of course, but over centuries the words have changed their meanings along with

the buildings: original houses have grown upwards, and the gardens have been reduced to the alleys buried beneath them.

Riddle's Court could have been just one of them had it not been that, about halfway through its history, the Bailie John McMorran decided to disrupt that pattern and to build himself not a tenement, or land, but a little palace, around a courtyard.

It was a gesture that took Riddle's Court on a very different journey to its neighbours. Over the centuries it's become a banqueting house, a palace for a great princess, a slum, a library, a summer school, a place for protest and ultimately, like the stories of the unreliable guide, and like the Ghost Room itself, a meeting place of past, present and future.

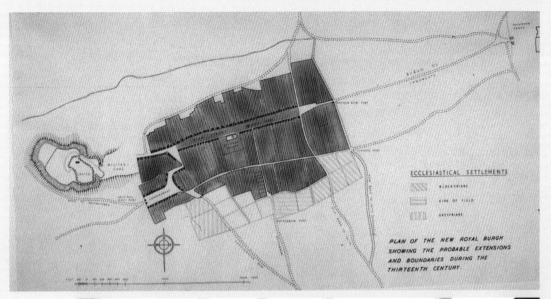

Top. The original pattern of
properties: Edinburgh in the
thirteenth century, imagined
by Sir Frank Mears in the
twentieth.

Above. A typical tenement
and a typical close: Riddle's
Court on the Royal Mile.

NOTES

Introduction: *An Unreliable Guide*

p.5 *'points out the very spot where the Bailie breathed his last...'*
W. G. Burn Murdoch, *From Edinburgh to the Antarctic*
(London: Longmans, Green and Co., 1894), pp. 11–12

Chapter 1: *A Ghost Room*

p.11 *'Conserving the Past: Building the Future'* http://
www.shbt.org.uk/about-us (accessed February 2018)

Chapter 2: *A Library, and a Book*

p.16 *'develop educational opportunities for the most disadvantaged'*
WEA website, Who We Are (accessed February 2018)

p.16 *'bath nights meant that cold water had to be heated on the gas
hob'* John Middlemiss, 'Living in Riddle's Court 1945–55'
in Elizabeth Bryan and Alicia Bruce (eds) *Vivendo
Discimus: By Living We Learn – The Life and Times of
Riddle's Court, 1590–2007* (Edinburgh: Workers'
Education Association, 2007), p. 46.

p.17 *'Centrally situated, and well equipped with gracious rooms of
various sizes...'* Elizabeth Bryan and Alicia Bruce (eds)
*Vivendo Discimus: By Living We Learn – The Life and
Times of Riddle's Court, 1590–2007* (Edinburgh: Workers'
Education Association, 2007), p. 50.

p.18 *'a Living Museum, as Patrick Geddes would have envisaged'*
Elizabeth Bryan and Alicia Bruce (eds) *Vivendo Discimus:
By Living We Learn – The Life and Times of Riddle's Court,
1590–2007* (Edinburgh: Workers' Education Association,
2007), p. 67.

p.18 *'those selling it and any future owners were made aware of its
significance'* Joyce Connon, introduction to Elizabeth
Bryan and Alicia Bruce (eds), *Vivendo Discimus: By
Living We Learn – The Life and Times of Riddle's Court,
1590–2007* (Edinburgh: Workers' Education Association,
2007).

p.18 *'They did not call in a team of professional historians...'*
Joyce Connon, introduction to Elizabeth Bryan and
Alicia Bruce (eds), *Vivendo Discimus: By Living We
Learn – The Life and Times of Riddle's Court, 1590–2007*
(Edinburgh: Workers' Education Association 2007).

p.19 *'Riddle's Court and Riddle's Close / (Old Stone, New Wood)*
Wendy Jones, 'Riddle's Court and Riddle's Close', in
Elizabeth Bryan and Alicia Bruce (eds) *Vivendo Discimus:
By Living We Learn – The Life and Times of Riddle's Court,
1590–2007* (Edinburgh: Workers' Education Association,
2007).

Chapter 3: *A Painted Ceiling*

p.24 *'a sort of co-operative society, a kind of Anarchist community
...'* 'A "Master Builder" – A Chat with Professor Geddes',
The Sketch (no. 114, Vol. 9, 3 April 1895), p. 514.

p.24 *'afforded by the unconscious mental giving and taking...'*
Geddes, quoted in Andrew Wright, *Riddle's Court,
Edinburgh* Conservation Statement (Edinburgh:
Cockburn Conservation Trust, 2008), p. 31.

p.26 *'devoted to a burlesque study of Primitive Man...'* Geddes
Archive at the University of Strathclyde Archive, T-GED
12/2/46, quoted in Michael Cressey, Charles McKean and
Alasdair Ross, *Riddle's Court, Lawnmarket, Edinburgh.*
Historic Building Survey Report No. 2164 (CFA
Archaeology Ltd, August 2012), p. 108.

p.26 *'Our true University is thus in the city'* Patrick Geddes,
'Paris University', unpublished manuscript, Rutgers
University Library, New Brunswick, New Jersey, quoted
in Helen Meller, *Patrick Geddes: Social Evolutionist and
City Planner* (Routledge, 1990), p. 34.

p.26 *'Thought does not exist by and for itself'* Patrick Geddes,
*Report on Edinburgh Summer Meeting, Eighth session,
August 6 31 1894* (Strathclyde University Geddes Archive,
T-GED 7/8/21), pp. 14–15.

p.26 *'access 17,000 books for the small sum of a shilling a month'*
Newspaper clipping, in Louise Forsyth, *Riddle's Court: The
Thomas Bonner Ceiling Deciphered* (unpublished, 2012), p. 7.

p.26 *'has done and is doing good work'* Newspaper clipping, in
Louis Forsyth, *Riddle's Court: The Thomas Bonner Ceiling
Deciphered* (unpublished, 2012), p. 7.

p.26 *'He did not claim superior intelligence...'* Newspaper
clipping, in Louis Forsyth, *Riddle's Court: The Thomas
Bonner Ceiling Deciphered* (unpublished, 2012), p. 7.

p.27 *'renewed usefulness and beauty'* Geddes: Competition submission for Dunfermline, 1904, quoted in Andrew Wright, *Riddle's Court, Edinburgh*, Conservation Statement (Edinburgh: Cockburn Conservation Trust, 2008), p. 32.

Chapter 4: *Window Seats*

p.31 *'enlarging and greatly improving that fine old building'* Edinburgh Commissioners Plans and Works Minute Book Vol. II – SLG63/1G, 20 February 1836, quoted in Michael Cressey, Charles McKean and Alasdair Ross *Riddle's Court, Lawnmarket, Edinburgh* Historic Building Survey (Edinburgh: CFA, 2013), p. 118

p.31 *'scandalous inconveniences'* Daniel Defoe, 'A Journey Round the Island of Great Britain', 1707, quoted in Andrew Wright, *Riddle's Court, Edinburgh* Conservation Statement (Edinburgh: Cockburn Conservation Trust, 2008), p. 21.

Chapter 5: *A Winding Stair*

p.35 *'They never try to live among these fragments...'* Lord Cockburn, 'Memorials', quoted in Andrew Wright, *Riddle's Court, Edinburgh* Conservation Statement (Edinburgh: Cockburn Conservation Trust, 2008), p. 23.

p.35 *'the wreck and rubbish of past centuries...'* Burn and Hamilton, quoted in Andrew Wright, *Riddle's Court, Edinburgh* Conservation Statement (Edinburgh: Cockburn Conservation Trust, 2008), p. 24.

p.36 *'the most squalid conglomeration...'* Geddes, 1915, quoted in Andrew Wright, *Riddle's Court, Edinburgh* Conservation Statement (Edinburgh: Cockburn Conservation Trust, 2008), p. 27.

p.37 *'could never think of going into a neighbour's house...'* Gaynors (unpublished, Riddle's Court archive), Book 1

p.37 *'the real church'* Gaynors, Book 1

p.37 *'it was deemed advisable to stop here.'* Gaynors, Book 3

p.37 *'come down in the world they rise in the stair'* Gaynors, Book 5

p.37 *'husband has been drinking, takes things out of the house...'* Gaynors, Book 7

p.38 *'I looked at him, and it was true enough...'* Gaynors, Book 2

p.38 *The 1881 census records, at the same time, 247 inhabitants.* Elizabeth Bryan and Alicia Bruce (eds) *Vivendo Discimus: By Living We Learn – The Life and Times of Riddle's Court 1590–2007* (Edinburgh: Workers' Education Association, 2007)

p.39 *'Do you wonder Edinburgh is renowned for its medical schools?'* 'Account of a Whirlwind Tour with Patrick Geddes in the Rain', quoted in Philip Boardman, *The Worlds of Patrick Geddes: Biologist, Town Planner, Re-educator, Peace Warrior* (1978), p. 146

Chapter 6: *A Panelled Room*

p.41 *'a fishcadger occupied the Royal Apartment...'* Quoted in Andrew Wright, *Riddle's Court, Edinburgh* Conservation Statement (Edinburgh: Cockburn Conservation Trust, 2008), p. 25.

p.43 *'a head, viz., myself, and two inferior member...'* David Hume, 'Letter to Dr. John Clephane', quoted in Elizabeth Bryan and Alicia Bruce (eds), *Vivendo Discimus: By Living We Learn – The Life and Times of Riddle's Court, 1590–2007* (Edinburgh: Workers' Education Association, 2007)

p.44 *'He was a lovely person, had a vertuous & excellent Lady'* John Evelyn, quoted in http://www.campin.me.uk/ Dalkeith/Scotts/Scotts.htm (accessed February 2018)

Chapter 7: *Bailie and Banquet*

p.52 *'It opened in four quarters, and from it emerged the provost's son'* Amy Juhala, *The Court of King James VI of Scotland 1567 1603* (PhD thesis, published 2000) https://www.era.lib.ed.ac.uk/handle/1842/1727 (accessed February 2018), pp. 192–202

p.52 *'He'd come on a diplomatic mission...'* Extracted from Michael Pearce, *The Riddle's Court Banquet and Scottish Diplomacy in 1598* (unpublished, 2011)

p.52 *'fowls wylde and tame'* Extracted from Frances Mercer, 'The Banquet for the Duke of Holstein' in Elizabeth Bryan and Alicia Bruce (eds) *Vivendo Discimus: By Living We Learn – The Life and Times of Riddle's Court, 1590–2007* (Edinburgh: Workers Education Association, 2007)

p.53 *'Timber was brought up from Leith, along with 600 nails...'* Extracted from Frances Mercer, 'The Banquet for the Duke of Holstein', in Elizabeth Bryan and Alicia Bruce (eds), *Vivendo Discimus: By Living We Learn – The Life and Times of Riddle's Court, 1590–2007* (Edinburgh: Workers Education Association, 2007)

p.54 *'McMorane came wi armed men'* Frances Mercer, 'The Ballad O' Bailie McMorran', in Elizabeth Bryan and Alicia Bruce (eds), *Vivendo Discimus: By Living We Learn – The Life and Times of Riddle's Court, 1590 2007* (Edinburgh: Workers' Education Association, 2007)

p.54 *There were musical instruments, 'hagbuttis', two cutlasses and a short sword...'* John Mcmorran's Inventory of his Goods and his Gear', quoted in Michael Cressey, Charles McKean and Alasdair Ross *Riddle's Court, Lawnmarket, Edinburgh* Historic Building Survey (Edinburgh: CFA, 2013), p. 89.

p.55 *George blocked up the entrance to the courtyard with a timber 'ravel'...* 'John Mcmorran's Inventory of his Goods and his Gear', quoted in Michael Cressey, Charles McKean and Alasdair Ross *Riddle's Court, Lawnmarket, Edinburgh* Historic Building Survey (Edinburgh: CFA, 2013), p. 11.

p.55 *In 1639, George took his neighbours to court* 'John Mcmorran's Inventory of his Goods and his Gear', quoted in Michael Cressey, Charles McKean and Alasdair Ross *Riddle's Court, Lawnmarket, Edinburgh* Historic Building Survey (Edinburgh: CFA, 2013), p. 11.

Chapter 8: *The Ghost Room, Again*

p.57 *Above the bairns was a 'high chamber'* Michael Pearce, *The Rooms of John McMorran* (unpublished)

ACKNOWLEDGEMENTS

I would like to acknowledge the support and help provided by a wide range of people in researching and producing this book: the Scottish Historic Buildings Trust, notably Russell Clegg, Una Richards, Marilyne MacLaren and John Lowry; Audrey Dakin, Historic Environment Scotland; National Museum of Scotland; National Galleries of Scotland; National Libraries of Scotland; University of Edinburgh Archives, and Andrew Simmons, Deborah Warner and Hugh Andrew at Birlinn Ltd.

I would also like to thank many without whose engagements this building's story would not be what it is: Michael Pearce, the Workers' Education Association, FORCE, Stuart Kelly, Lou Rosenberg, Silvia Ojeda Garcia, and the many Edinburgh College of Art students with whom, over a decade, I have worked on Riddle's Court.

PICTURE CREDITS